HEINEMANN ELT GUIDED READERS

INTERMEDIATE LEVEL

FREDERICK FORSYTH

Used in Evidence and Other Stories

Retold by Stephen Colbourn

HEINEMANN ELT

HEINEMANN ELT GUIDED READERS
INTERMEDIATE LEVEL

Series Editor: John Milne

The Heinemann ElT Guided Readers provide a choice of enjoyable reading material for learners of English. The series is published at five levels – Starter, Beginner, Elementary, Intermediate and Upper. At **Intermediate Level**, the control of content and language has the following main features:

Information Control

Information which is vital to the understanding of the story is presented in an easily assimilated manner and is repeated when necessary. Difficult allusion and metaphor are avoided and cultural backgrounds are made explicit.

Structure Control

Most of the structures used in the Readers will be familiar to students who have completed an elementary course of English. Other grammatical features may occur, but their use is made clear through context and re-inforcement. This ensures that the reading, as well as being enjoyable, provides a continual learning situation for the students. Sentences are limited in most cases to a maximum of three clauses and within sentences there is a balanced use of adverbial and adjectival phrases. Great care is taken with pronoun reference.

Vocabulary Control

There is a basic vocabulary of approximately 1600 words. Help is given to the students in the form of illustrations, which are closely related to the text.

Glossary

Some difficult words and phrases in this book are important for understanding the story. Some of these words are explained in the story, some are shown in the pictures, and others are marked with a number like this … [3]. Words with a number are explained in the Glossary on page 59.

Contents

A Note About These Stories

The stories in this book take place in four countries. *Used in Evidence* takes place in Dublin, in the Republic of Ireland. *There Are No Snakes in Ireland* takes place in Bangor and Belfast, in Northern Ireland and – for a few pages – in the city of Bombay, in India. *The Emperor* takes place on the island of Mauritius.

The island of Ireland is to the west of Great Britain. The island is divided into two countries. The larger one, the Republic of Ireland, is in the south. It is often called Eire, which is its Irish name. Eire was once part of the United Kingdom of Great Britain and Ireland. But Eire is now an independent country. Dublin is its capital city.

The other country on the island is Northern Ireland, which is often called Ulster. Ulster is part of the United Kingdom of Great Britain and Northern Ireland. Belfast is the capital city and Bangor is a town near Belfast.

For many years, there was fighting in Northern Ireland. The fighting was between people who wanted Northern Ireland to join the Republic and people who wanted the country to remain part of the United Kingdom. There are famous universities in both Dublin and Belfast.

There is a strange thing about Ireland – no snakes live there. There are snakes in England and Scotland and Wales, the countries of Great Britain. But there are no snakes on the island of Ireland. There is a very old story about this. Long ago – in about the year 400 AD – a holy man came to Ireland. He was Saint Patrick. He came to teach the people about Christianity. At that time, there were many snakes in Ireland. Saint Patrick quickly destroyed all the snakes except

4

one. The saint could not catch this clever old snake. So Patrick made a beautiful box and he showed it to the old snake. He invited the snake to look inside the box. The snake got into the box and Saint Patrick quickly shut the lid. Then he threw the box and the snake into the sea. So now people say that there are no snakes in Ireland because Saint Patrick killed all of them.

Bombay is a great city on the west coast of India. It is India's largest city and it is an important sea-port. About twelve million people live there. In 1995, the city was given a new name. It is now called Mumbai.

Mauritius is a small island in the Indian Ocean. It is to the east of Madagascar, the large island on the south-eastern side of Africa. The people of Mauritius speak English, French and Creole – a language with very many French words. Mauritius has a tropical climate and many beautiful beaches. There are coral reefs round the island.

Many tourists visit Mauritius. And many of them enjoy water-sports and sea-fishing. Some people like to go out in boats and catch fish such as sharks, marlins, tuna, bonitos and dorados. This is called game-fishing. The big fish in the story, *The Emperor*, is a marlin. Marlins are very large fish, sometimes 2.5m long. They have strong tails, tall fins on their backs and long, sharp spikes on their heads.

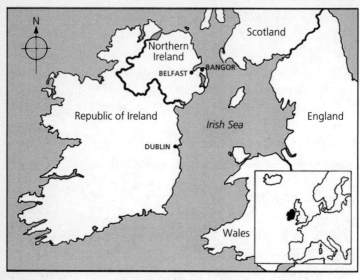

Map of Ireland

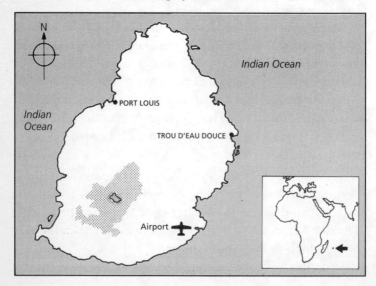

Map of Mauritius

USED IN EVIDENCE[1]

In the 1970s, many new houses and apartments were built in Dublin. In some parts of the city, the old houses were very bad. Dublin City Council[2] knocked down[3] these bad homes. The council built new houses and apartments for the people who lived in the old houses.

The worst houses were in Mayo Road. These houses were more than a hundred years old. Rain came in through the roofs. The walls were damp. People did not want to live in these old buildings any more.

In 1978, Dublin City Council built some new apartments near Mayo Road. The City Council bought the old houses in the road from their owners. The people moved out of their old houses and into the new apartments. Council workmen started to knock down the old buildings. The council was going to build a new shopping centre with a large car park in Mayo Road.

———

The council knocked down all the houses in Mayo Road – except one. One old man did not want to move out of his home. The council sent him many letters, but he refused to leave. At last, the council asked the police to help them. They asked the police to get the old man out of his house.

———

It was nine o'clock on a wet November morning. The sky was grey and the rain was falling heavily. The rain fell on the building site[4] where the houses of Mayo Road had stood. The rain fell on the tarmac[5] of the road and it fell on the only house which remained – Number 38.

A police car came along Mayo Road. There were two

7

men in the car – the young police driver and Chief Superintendent Hanley. Bill Hanley was in charge of[6] all the policemen in this part of Dublin.

The car stopped outside 38 Mayo Road and the chief superintendent looked around him. A year ago, there had been houses on both sides of the street. But now only one house remained. Number 38 stood alone in the middle of the large muddy[7] building site. The old man was still inside the house.

A big crowd of people was standing a few metres from the house. When they saw the police car, the people moved forward. There were council officials, council social workers[8], and council workmen in the crowd. The officials were from the Housing Department[9]. They had asked the police to get the old man out of Number 38. The social workers were going to help the old man to move into his new home. Then the workmen were going to knock down the house.

Chief Superintendent Hanley got out of the police car and spoke to the officials from the City Council.

'Have you talked to the old man in the house?' the Chief Superintendent asked.

'Mr Larkin won't speak to us,' one of the officials replied. 'We've tried to speak to him. We've told him that he must leave before nine o'clock this morning.'

Hanley looked at the crowd. He saw two newspaper reporters. One of them had a camera.

Hanley thought about the front page of tomorrow's newspaper. 'There will be a picture of the old man coming out of the house with two policemen,' he thought. 'And there will be a headline above the picture – POLICE TAKE OLD MAN FROM HIS HOME.'

Bill Hanley spoke to one of the officials.

'I don't like this part of my job,' he said, 'but I have to do it.'

'The City Council has sent many letters to Mr Larkin,' the official said. 'We have told him that he must move out. We have told him that the council has bought his house and built a new apartment for him. But he hasn't replied to any of the letters.'

Chief Superintendent Hanley looked at his watch. The time was two minutes past nine. 'Speak to the old man again,' he said to the council officials.

The Chief Housing Officer from the council knocked on the door of 38 Mayo Road.

'Mr Larkin!' he shouted. There was no answer.

'Mr Larkin!' the Chief Housing Officer shouted again, 'we have an order from the court[10]. If you don't come out, we'll knock down the door.'

But there was still no reply.

Hanley spoke to two workmen who were holding large hammers.

'Knock down the door,' he said.

The workmen went to the front door. They broke the door with their hammers. Mr Larkin had put a table and some chairs against the inside of the door but the workmen quickly pushed the furniture away. They walked into the house.

Hanley spoke to the social workers. 'Go in now, please,' he said.

The social workers followed the workmen into the house. A few minutes later, they were leading Mr Larkin out through the broken front door.

The social workers led Mr Larkin out of the house.

Mr Larkin was a pale, thin old man. He was ill and hungry and his hands were shaking. Bill Hanley felt sorry for him. A social worker put a woollen blanket round the old man's shoulders. The social workers were going to take Mr Larkin to his new council apartment. But Hanley had an idea.

'Put Mr Larkin in the police car,' he said. 'We'll give him a good meal before he goes to his new home. There's a café near here.'

'OK, Chief Superintendent,' said one of the social workers. 'We'll wait in our car while Mr Larkin is eating. It's a cold morning.'

As the police took Mr Larkin to the café, the workmen were carrying the old man's furniture out of the house. Soon, all the furniture was gone.

The workmen opened the back door of the house. Behind Number 38 Mayo Road, there was a small garden. The workmen found two chickens in a shed in the garden.

'The old man can't have chickens in his new apartment,' said one of the men. 'I'll take these home with me. I have a little garden. I keep chickens too.'

At half-past ten, the council workmen began to knock down the walls of the old house.

———

In the café, Bill Hanley bought Mr Larkin a meal of eggs and toast and tea. And he bought a cup of tea for himself and for his driver. The old man ate the food. He did not speak. Hanley and the police driver were drinking their tea when another police car stopped outside the café.

A policeman came into the café and spoke to the chief superintendent.

'Will you come back to Mayo Road, sir?' he said. 'The

workmen have found something.'

The old man stopped eating and looked at Hanley.

The chief superintendent stood up. 'You stay here with Mr Larkin,' he said to his driver.

He left the café and returned with the other policeman to Mayo Road.

The crowd was still standing outside Number 38. A man in the crowd called out, 'Is there some treasure in there? Is that why the old man wouldn't leave? Have you found some money?'

Hanley went into the house. The workmen had started to knock down the fireplace and the chimney[11]. Bricks from the wall were lying on the floor. The workmen had made a large hole in a wall by the fireplace and they had found something behind the wall. They had seen something through the hole. They had seen something between the wall and the chimney.

'Look in there, sir!' one of the workmen said, as Hanley came into the room.

Hanley looked through the hole. Between the wall and the chimney, he saw a human body. It was old and black, but he saw that it was the body of a woman.

Hanley went outside to the police car. He made a call on the car's radio. He called Police Headquarters and he spoke to an inspector.

'I've found the body of a woman in Mayo Road,' Hanley said. 'She was behind a wall. She has been there for some years. I think that the woman was murdered. Please send someone to take the body to the mortuary[12]. There will be a murder investigation[13].'

'Do you have a suspect[14]?' asked the other man.

Between the wall and the chimney,
Hanley saw a human body.

'Yes,' Hanley answered. 'Mr Larkin, the owner of 38 Mayo Road. I'm taking him to the police station now.'

The police car took Hanley back to the café. He went inside and he spoke quietly to Mr Larkin.

'We've found her,' he said. 'You must come with me to the police station.'

The old man followed Hanley to the police car. He did not speak.

When they were in the car, Hanley asked Mr Larkin a question.

'Who is the dead woman in your house?' he asked.

The old man refused to say anything.

'Is it Mrs Larkin?' Hanley asked. 'We will find out soon. Aren't you worried? You'll feel better if you tell us about it.'

But the old man would not speak.

When they arrived at the police station, Hanley put Larkin into an interview room[15]. He gave the old man some tea and some cigarettes. Mr Larkin drank the tea and took the cigarettes but still he did not speak.

'I'll talk to you later, Mr Larkin,' said Hanley.

Hanley went to his office and he phoned the police pathologist[16]. The pathologist looked at dead bodies and found out information about them. Now he would help Hanley by looking at this body – he would do a post-mortem examination[17].

'I'm going to send the body of a woman to the mortuary,' Hanley said. 'I want to know *how* the woman died and I want to know *when* she died. I need the information as soon as possible, please. This is a murder investigation.'

Next, Bill Hanley spoke to a police sergeant.

'Go to the council offices,' Hanley told the sergeant. 'Find out how many years Mr Larkin lived in Mayo Road. Also, try to find out who lived in the house before Mr Larkin.'

Then Hanley sent another sergeant to Mayo Road.

'Find out if the old man left any papers or documents in his house,' Hanley told the sergeant. 'Also, find out the names of his neighbours – the other people who lived in Mayo Road before the houses were knocked down. Talk to them. Ask them if Larkin was married.'

———

Early in the afternoon, the pathologist phoned Hanley.

'The body from Mayo Road is a mummy[18],' the pathologist said.

'What do you mean – a mummy?' asked Hanley.

'The dead body was between a wall and the chimney,' the pathologist replied. 'For years, the heat and smoke from the fireplace has dried the body. The body is like an Egyptian mummy.'

'That's interesting,' said Hanley. 'But can you tell me *how* the woman died? And can you tell me *when* she died?'

'No. I can't tell you that today,' answered the pathologist. 'I have to do a post-mortem examination on the body. I think that the woman was strangled. I think that something was tied tightly round her neck. I think that the woman died many years ago, but I am not sure about that. I will have more information for you after the post-mortem.'

'When will you be able to give me the information?' Hanley asked. 'I need some help with this investigation.'

'The body is hard and dry,' said the pathologist. 'I'll have to make the body soft. I'll have to soak it. I'll leave the body in some liquid until the morning. I'll do the post-mortem tomorrow, when the body is soft.'

Hanley thanked the pathologist and he put down the phone. A few minutes later, one of the police sergeants brought him some more news.

'Sir, we've found some documents at 38 Mayo Road,' he said. 'We've found some papers. There is some information about the house in them. And we've found a British Army pay book and a photograph. Here they are.' He put a large envelope on Hanley's desk.

These things gave Hanley a lot of information and he made notes as he looked at them.

First, he looked at the army pay book. Every soldier in the British Army had a pay book. It showed how much money the soldier had been paid while he was in the army. And it showed the soldier's date of birth and his army number. Every soldier in the British Army had a number. The pay book which Hanley was holding had belonged to Herbert James Larkin. Larkin was an Irishman. He had been born in Dublin, in 1911. But he had been in the British Army from 1940 to 1946.

Hanley phoned the British Embassy[19] in Dublin. He spoke to the military attaché[20] at the embassy. Hanley told the attaché Larkin's army number and he asked the attaché to get some more information about Larkin.

'I'll check the Army's files,' said the military attaché. 'I'll phone Army Headquarters in London. I'll call you tomorrow, when I have some news.'

Next, Hanley looked at the papers. They were the deeds[21] of 38 Mayo Road. These papers told Hanley that Larkin had bought the house in 1954. Now, Hanley wanted to know where Larkin had lived between 1946 and 1954.

The chief superintendent phoned an official at the City Council.

'I want to find out about Herbert James Larkin who lived at 38 Mayo Road,' said Hanley. 'Please give me any information that you have.'

The official asked Hanley to wait while he got some files. After a minute he spoke again.

'From 1946 to 1954, Mr Larkin lived in North London,' said the council official. 'He returned to Ireland in 1954. He was a security guard[22] in Dublin from 1954 to 1976. Mr Larkin retired[23] in 1976.'

Hanley thanked the official and he put down the phone. Then he looked at the photograph. It was many years old. It showed a soldier and a young woman. The man was Larkin. He was dressed in army uniform. Who was the woman? Was it Larkin's wife?

———

Later that day, the sergeant who had been to speak to Mr Larkin's neighbours came to see Hanley.

'I've spoken to some of the people who used to live in Mayo Road,' the sergeant said. 'I spoke to a woman called Mrs Moran. She lived next to the Larkins and she remembers the time when they moved into Number 38.'

'So, Larkin *was* married,' said Hanley.

'Yes, sir,' said the sergeant. 'And Mrs Moran remembers the man who lived at Number 38 before the Larkins. That man's wife was dead when Mrs Moran moved to Mayo Road. The man himself died in 1954. Five weeks after the man died, the Larkins moved into the house. Mrs Moran said that Mr Larkin was about forty-five years old at that time. But his wife was nearly twenty years younger than him. Mrs Moran said that Mrs Larkin was English – she came from London.'

'And what happened to Mrs Larkin?' Hanley asked.

'Mrs Moran says that Mrs Larkin disappeared late in 1963.'

'Disappeared? Is Mrs Moran certain about the date?'

'Yes,' replied the sergeant. 'She said that Mrs Larkin disappeared in the autumn of 1963. She had disappeared before President John F. Kennedy[24] was killed in November 1963.'

'Was Mrs Moran worried when Mrs Larkin disappeared?'

'I don't think that she was worried,' the sergeant said.

'Mrs Larkin had an argument with her husband and she disappeared. The neighbours thought that she had gone back to London.'

'Sergeant, *I* think that Larkin killed his wife,' said Hanley. 'I think that he hid her body. That's why Larkin didn't want to move out of 38 Mayo Road. He knew that someone would find the body when the house was knocked down. That's why he didn't want the council workmen to knock down the house.'

'I think that you're right, sir,' said the sergeant.

Hanley went to the interview room and sat down opposite Mr Larkin. The old man looked very worried.

'Mr Larkin, we know that your wife disappeared in 1963 – fifteen years ago,' said Hanley. 'Tell me what happened. You knew that someone would find your wife's body one day. Now we *have* found it. You *must* speak to me. This is a murder investigation, Mr Larkin. Now, tell me about your wife. You'll feel much better!'

Larkin said nothing.

'Was the woman behind the wall in the house your wife, Mr Larkin?' asked Hanley.

Larkin looked at the chief superintendent for a moment. Then he smiled. Suddenly his eyes were bright and calm. But still he said nothing.

'Herbert James Larkin,' said Hanley. 'I charge you with[25] the murder of your wife. You do not have to say anything. But anything that you *do* say will be written down. It will be used in evidence in a court of law.'

———

The next morning, Hanley waited for a phone call from the pathologist. But the first call that he received was from an official at the City Council.

'Chief Superintendent Hanley, your men are stopping our work at Mayo Road,' said the council official. 'We want to cover the ground with concrete[26] and tarmac. The building site is going to be a shopping centre and a car park. There is a lot of work to do. Can we start work today?'

'Yes, OK,' said Hanley. 'We've looked at the house. You can knock down all the walls now. You can build your shopping centre. You can make your car park.'

Twenty minutes later, Hanley received the phone call from the pathologist.

'I'm going to start the post-mortem examination now,'

said the pathologist. 'I'll call you again in a few hours.'

While Hanley was waiting, the military attaché at the British Embassy phoned. He gave Hanley some information about Larkin's life in the British Army.

'Herbert James Larkin joined the army in 1940,' said the attaché, Major Dawkins. 'Mr Larkin fought in the Second World War[27]. He fought in Egypt in 1941. The German Army captured Larkin at the end of 1941 and he was taken to a prison camp[28] in Poland. He was at that camp until 1945.'

'Thank you, Major Dawkins,' said Hanley. 'Do you have any information about Larkin's marriage?'

'Yes, I do,' said Major Dawkins. 'Mr Larkin was still in the army when he got married. He got married in London, in November 1945. His wife's name was Violet Mary Smith. She was seventeen years old and she worked in a hotel in London.'

Hanley thanked Major Dawkins again and said goodbye to him. Then he waited for the pathologist to phone again.

'So, Violet Smith married a man who was more than twice her age,' Bill Hanley said to himself. 'When Violet disappeared in 1963, she was thirty-five years old and Herbert Larkin was fifty-two.'

The phone rang. 'Hanley, I've found out how the woman died,' said the pathologist. 'She *was* murdered. Someone hit on her the head and then strangled her.'

Hanley wrote down the information. 'Thank you,' he said. 'Can you tell me when she died now?'

'The body had been in the house for more than thirty years,' said the pathologist. 'The woman died between 1940 and 1945.'

'But the Larkins did not move to 38 Mayo Road until

1954,' said Hanley.

'I'm telling you what I have found out, Hanley,' replied the pathologist.

'And how old was the woman when she died?' asked Hanley.

'She was more than fifty years old,' said the pathologist.

Chief Superintendent Hanley put down the phone. Then he spoke to the sergeant who had talked to Mrs Moran.

'Sergeant, who was the man who lived at 38 Mayo Road before the Larkins?' Hanley asked.

'I couldn't find out his name, sir,' answered the sergeant. 'But I know that the man lived alone. His wife was dead.'

'Yes,' said Hanley. 'It was *his* wife's body in the house! Let Mr Larkin go, sergeant. Let him go to his new apartment. Tell the social workers at the City Council that the old man is free. Tell them that Mr Larkin isn't a murderer. The City Council must take care of him now!'

———

That afternoon, Mr Larkin moved into his new apartment. But a few days later, he wanted to visit Mayo Road.

The old man walked to Mayo Road. His house was no longer there. The council workmen had knocked down all the walls and they had covered the ground with concrete. When Mr Larkin arrived, the foreman[29] was walking round the building site. He was looking at the new concrete. He was finding out if the concrete had become hard.

'What's this?' he called to one of his men. He pointed to a piece of concrete which was a different colour. 'This piece of concrete is old.'

Mr Larkin watched the two men carefully.

'There was a chicken shed in the back garden of Number

22

38,' said the workman. 'This concrete was the floor of the chicken shed. The old concrete is very hard and strong, so we put new concrete around it.'

'OK,' said the foreman. He called to the driver of a bull-dozer[30]. 'Cover all this concrete with tarmac!' he shouted.

The bulldozer pushed soft, hot tarmac over the concrete.
Mr Larkin watched the black tarmac covering the floor of his chicken shed. Then the old man smiled and he started to walk back to his new home.

THE EMPEROR

'Roger, I'm not going to like this place,' said Edna Murgatroyd.

'What's wrong, Edna?' asked her husband.

There was always something wrong! Mrs Edna Murgatroyd was always complaining. The Murgatroyds had been married for twenty-five years and Edna was never happy about anything or anybody.

'It's hot and dirty here,' she said.

'Yes, dear,' said Roger Murgatroyd, 'but we're only going to stay here for a week.'

An hour earlier, the Murgatroyds had arrived here on the island of Mauritius. Now they were in a taxi, travelling north from the airport towards Trou d'Eau Douce – a village on the east coast of the island.

There were three passengers in the taxi – Roger Murgatroyd, Edna Murgatroyd and John Higgins.

Roger Murgatroyd was about fifty years old. He was short, he was fat and he wore glasses. Today, he was wearing a dark suit. His wife was a few years younger than Roger but she was heavy too. She was wearing a large, dark red dress. John Higgins was about twenty-five years old. He was wearing a cool white suit and sunglasses.

The two men worked for the Midland Bank. Roger Murgatroyd and John Higgins were the Midland Bank's Employees[31] of the Year.

Every year, the bank rewarded two of its employees. The two employees who had worked the hardest were given a reward. The bank gave the two employees and their families a holiday. This year, 1977, the reward was a holiday in Mauritius. Edna Murgatroyd had come to Mauritius with her husband. John Higgins was not married – he was travelling alone.

The taxi passed through the village of Trou d'Eau Douce. It was a pretty village beside the sea. The village had a small harbour. There were some fishing boats in the harbour.

'This is a good place for game-fishing,' said Higgins.

After a few more miles, the taxi arrived at the Hotel St Geran. It was a beautiful white building near the sea.

Higgins and the Murgatroyds got out of the taxi and Higgins paid the driver. Two hotel porters carried the three travellers' bags to the reception desk. The manager of the hotel welcomed the new guests in the reception area.

'I hope that you enjoy your holiday,' he said. 'Mauritius is a beautiful island.'

Suddenly, a man who was wearing shorts[32] and a brightly-coloured shirt walked towards the desk. He was holding a can of beer. He had come from the hotel bar, which was near the reception area. He looked at John Higgins and the Murgatroyds.

'Are you the new guests?' he asked in a loud voice. He spoke with an Australian accent[33].

'Mmmm. Yes,' said Roger Murgatroyd. Roger was a shy man – he could never think of anything to say to strangers.

'I'm from Sydney, Australia,' said the man. 'My name's Harry Foster, what's *your* name?'

'I'm Murgatroyd – Roger Murgatroyd. This is my wife – Edna, and this is my colleague[34], John Higgins.'

Edna Murgatroyd looked angrily at the Australian's shirt and his can of beer. She did not speak.

'Are you the new guests?' the man asked.

'Where are you from?' asked Harry Foster. He was asking them which country they came from but Roger did not understand.

'The Midland,' he said. 'Higgins is from the Midland's head office and I'm from a branch[35] of the bank in East London.'

Harry Foster laughed. 'So – Murgatroyd of the Midland and Higgins from Head Office,' he said. 'I like it. Good on yer[36], Murgatroyd!'

The hotel manager looked at Edna Murgatroyd's angry face. He spoke quickly.

'Please let our new guests relax after their long journey, Mr Foster,' he said. He held Harry Foster's arm and led him back towards the bar.

Edna stared at the Australian. 'That man is drunk!' she said loudly.

'He's on holiday,' said her husband.

'I don't like people who get drunk!' said Edna.

When they got to their room, Edna Murgatroyd decided to sleep for an hour after the long journey. Roger Murgatroyd was pleased. He sat quietly and looked out of the window.

———

The next day, Roger Murgatroyd began to enjoy his holiday. When he woke up, he looked out of the bedroom window. The view was beautiful.

When he looked out of his bedroom window at home in London, he saw cold, grey, wet streets. But here, in Mauritius, he could see the golden beach, the blue sea and the green palm trees. He looked at the hot sun and at the bright sea and at the white waves. He felt happy and relaxed.

Murgatroyd ate some fruit for breakfast. Then he went

down to the beach to swim and to lie in the sun. At ten
o'clock, Edna came down to the beach too. For the next two
hours, she sat under a sun umbrella and told her husband
what to do. She told him to bring cold drinks, then she said
that she did not like them. She told him to put sun-tan oil[37]
on her back, although she did not want to lie in the hot sun.

At lunch time, the Murgatroyds went back to their room.
Roger put on a pair of brightly-coloured shorts.

'Let's go to the restaurant,' he said.

'You can't wear those shorts,' his wife said. 'You must wear
a pair of trousers.'

'Yes, dear,' said Murgatroyd. He took off the shorts and put
on a pair of dark trousers.

———

The days passed quickly. Every day, the Murgatroyds did the
same things. They sat on the beach. Edna sat under a sun
umbrella and read romantic novels[38]. Roger did what his wife
told him to do.

John Higgins had met some young people and he went out
with them each day. The Murgatroyds did not see him often.
But on the Friday afternoon, Roger *did* see Higgins. Higgins
spoke quietly to Roger Murgatroyd while Edna was asleep.

'Tomorrow is the last day of our holiday,' said Higgins. 'Do
you want to come game-fishing?'

'What do you mean – fishing for sharks?' asked
Murgatroyd.

'Not sharks – tuna, bonito, dorado and other big fish,'
Higgins replied. 'I've been to the harbour at Trou d'Eau
Douce. Three South African businessmen hired[39] a boat.
They wanted to go fishing tomorrow. But now they have to
go back to Johannesburg quickly, so they don't have time for

fishing. The businessmen have paid half the money for the boat. So we can hire the boat for only fifty dollars. We can go game-fishing tomorrow.'

'Edna won't let me go,' said Murgatroyd sadly.

'Then don't tell her,' said Higgins. 'Just go!'

For a moment, Roger Murgatroyd was shocked. He always asked his wife before he did anything. But tomorrow was the last day of his holiday. He wanted to enjoy himself. He would never have a holiday like this one again. He wanted to go game-fishing with Higgins!

Suddenly, he felt happy. 'Edna will be angry,' he said to himself. 'Well, I don't care[40]!'

'Yes! All right,' he said to Higgins. 'I'll come with you.'

'Good!' said Higgins. 'Meet me by the hotel reception desk at four-thirty tomorrow morning.'

———

Murgatroyd was awake all night. He lay quietly beside his wife, but he did not sleep. At four o'clock, he got dressed quickly. He put on his brightly-coloured shorts and a thin shirt. It was dark outside. Murgatroyd left the bedroom very quietly and he met Higgins by the hotel reception desk. Soon they were in a taxi, travelling south towards Trou d'Eau Douce.

At the little harbour in Trou d'Eau Douce, they met their guide[41]. He was a tall South African called André Kilian. Murgatroyd and Higgins each gave him twenty-five dollars. The guide took them to a boat called the *Avant*. They met the captain and a young man who worked on the boat.

'This is Monsieur Patient,' said Kilian. 'And this is his grandson, Jean-Paul.'

Monsieur Patient was a strong old man in his seventies[42].

He was wearing an old straw hat. Jean-Paul was a tall man in his twenties.

Jean-Paul carried boxes of food and cans of beer onto the boat while his grandfather talked to Kilian. Finally, Jean-Paul put a large tool-box[43] and a metal bucket full of squid[44] onto the boat's wooden deck.

'We are ready to leave,' said Kilian.

———

At about half-past five, the boat left the harbour. The sun was rising.

André Kilian showed Murgatroyd and Higgins the two long fishing rods which were used to catch big fish. Each rod had a large reel[45] of very strong fishing line.

'The reels have eight hundred metres of line,' Kilian said. 'Big fish are very strong. A big fish will pull out several hundred metres of line from the reel. It's difficult to reel in a big fish. It's difficult to pull the fish to the boat.'

There was a special seat at the back of the *Avant*. A fishing rod could be fixed to the deck in front of the seat.

'When you catch a big fish, you must fix the rod here,' said the guide. He pointed at the deck. 'You must sit in this seat while you reel in the fish.'

At about half-past six, Monsieur Patient slowed down the boat's engine.

'We will fish here,' Kilian said.

Jean-Paul went to the fishing rods. At the end of each line, there was a very sharp hook. The young man put a small squid onto each hook, and he threw the ends of both lines into the sea. If a big fish ate one of the squid, the hook would cut into the fish's mouth. Then one of the fishermen could pull the fish to the boat. He could reel in the fish.

After a few minutes, one of the fishing lines became tight.
A fish had eaten the squid and the hook.

'We've caught a fish!' shouted Higgins. 'I'll reel it in!'

Higgins took the rod and he sat in the seat. He started to
reel in the fishing line. He turned the reel slowly and carefully. Soon, the fish was beside the boat. Jean-Paul leant

31

over the side of the *Avant*. He lifted the fish into the boat and pulled the hook out of its mouth.

'It's a bonito,' said Kilian. 'It weighs about two kilos.'

Jean-Paul put another squid on the hook and he threw it into the sea. Soon, one of the fishing lines was tight again. This time, Murgatroyd took the rod and sat in the seat. He started to turn the reel.

'It's heavy!' he said. 'It must be a big fish.'

He turned the reel slowly. He reeled in the fish. Kilian leant over the side of the boat and looked into the water.

'Another bonito,' said Kilian. 'A bigger one – about four or five kilos.'

———

At eight o'clock in the morning, the sun was getting hot. Higgins and Murgatroyd caught some more bonitos.

Before nine o'clock, Higgins caught a much larger fish. It was the colour of gold.

'It's a dorado,' said Kilian. 'Dorados are good to eat. We'll ask the chef at the Hotel St Geran to cook this fish tonight.'

Soon after nine o'clock, Monsieur Patient spoke to his grandson. He spoke in Creole French.

'Ya quelque chose – nous suit,' he said.

'What did he say?' asked Higgins.

'He said that there's something following us,' answered Kilian.

Higgins looked at the sea behind the boat. He could not see anything.

'How does he know?'

'Monsieur Patient has been fishing here, in this sea, for sixty years.'

Jean-Paul reeled in the lines. He took some wire-cutters[46] from the tool-box and he cut the hook from the end of each line. Then he fixed much larger hooks to the lines. He did not put squid on these. On each hook, he put one of the bonitos which they had caught.

Half an hour later, one of the lines became tight. Murgatroyd took the rod and sat in the seat. Suddenly, his line was pulled out very quickly. A hundred metres of line was pulled out in less than a minute. The reel made a loud noise as it went round and round.

'Hold onto the handle of the reel!' said Kilian. 'Slow down the reel, or all the line will be pulled off it. You've caught something big.'

Murgatroyd held the fishing rod tightly. He slowed down the reel. The end of the rod bent over and pointed down towards the sea. After three minutes, the reel stopped turning. Six hundred metres of fishing line had been pulled from the reel.

'We must put the harness on you,' said Kilian. 'This is a very big fish!'

The harness was fixed to the fishing seat. Quickly, Kilian and Jean-Paul harnessed Murgatroyd to the seat. There were two leather straps over his shoulders and two round his legs. Another strap was round his waist.

'Now the fish won't be able to pull you into the sea!' said Kilian.

Old Monsieur Patient slowly turned the boat. He looked at the sea behind the boat. 'Marlin!' he said.

'You're lucky, Mr Murgatroyd,' said Kilian, 'you've caught a marlin.'

'Is that good?' asked Murgatroyd.

'Marlin are the biggest and best game-fish,' Kilian

answered. 'Rich men come here every year. Many of them spend thousands of dollars and they never catch a marlin.'

Murgatroyd could not see the marlin, but he knew that it was very strong. Sometimes the fish turned and swam towards the boat. When that happened, Murgatroyd reeled in some of the line. Then the marlin turned away from the boat and pulled the line from the reel again.

'That fish will fight you for hours,' said Kilian.

Murgatroyd felt the heat of the sun. It was ten o'clock. His arms were aching. Soon the sun would be hotter. Could he hold the fishing rod for hours?

Between ten and eleven o'clock, Murgatroyd reeled in the line three times. Each time, he slowly and painfully reeled in a hundred metres of line. Each time, the big fish pulled a hundred metres out again.

At eleven o'clock, the marlin tail-walked for the first time. It was five hundred metres from the boat. It came out of the sea and it stood up on its tail.

'It's walking on the water!' said Murgatroyd.

Monsieur Patient looked at the huge fish. 'C'est l'Empereur,' he called to his grandson.

'What did he say?' asked Higgins.

'He said that it's the Emperor,' answered Kilian. 'All the fishermen on the island know about this fish. They say that the Emperor is the biggest blue marlin that they have ever seen.'

———

At midday, Murgatroyd was feeling tired and ill. His hands were very painful. He had been fighting the fish for two hours. Murgatroyd pulled. The fish pulled. Murgatroyd turned the reel forwards. The marlin made the reel turn

34

At eleven o'clock, the marlin tail-walked
for the first time.

backwards. Suddenly, the fish stopped pulling. A few minutes later, its head came out of the water. The fish was only three hundred metres from the boat. After a few seconds, it went back under the water.

'Reel in! Quickly! Reel in!' shouted Kilian.

Murgatroyd reeled in the line as fast as he could. His hands began to bleed[47].

'You're tired,' said Kilian. 'Shall I hold the rod for an hour? Then you can take it again.'

'How much longer will the marlin fight?' asked Murgatroyd.

Kilian looked at Monsieur Patient. The old man said, 'Deux heures encore.'

'Two more hours,' said Murgatroyd, 'I'm all right. I can do this for two more hours. It's *my* fish.'

Then the marlin started pulling on the line again, but it did not pull as strongly as before. For another ninety minutes the fish and the man fought each other. Murgatroyd's mouth and lips were dry. There was blood on the fishing rod. Pull. Reel. Pull. Reel. Murgatroyd forgot that his hands were bleeding.

At last, the marlin stopped pulling. Murgatroyd reeled in carefully. Suddenly they all saw the fish.

'The Emperor is coming in!' Kilian shouted.

The blue marlin came out of the water thirty metres from the boat. Murgatroyd continued to reel in the huge fish. When it was three metres away, he could see the hook in its mouth.

Jean-Paul moved to the side of the boat. He had a large, pointed metal bar his hand. He lifted the bar above his head. He was going to kill the fish.

'No!' shouted Murgatroyd.

Jean-Paul stopped and looked at Murgatroyd. Murgatroyd got out of the harness. Slowly and painfully, he went over to the tool-box. He took the wire-cutters from the tool-box and he walked to the side of the boat.

The huge blue body of the marlin lay in the water next to the boat. The fish was tired. It had no strength for fighting.

Murgatroyd leant over the side of the boat. He put the wire-cutters round the fishing line and he cut through it.

'What are you doing?' shouted Higgins. 'The Emperor will get away!'

'Yes,' said Murgatroyd.

The great Marlin went down slowly beneath the *Advant*. The fish was free.

Murgatroyd tried to stand up but he was too weak and dizzy[48]. He fell heavily onto the deck. He had fainted!

———

The *Avant* returned to the harbour at Trou d'Eau Douce in the evening. Murgatroyd had drunk some cold beer and he was feeling better. But his hands were still very painful. And the skin of his arms and his legs and his face was sunburnt.

There was a crowd of villagers standing at the harbour when Monsieur Patient turned off the *Avant's* engine. Jean-Paul and his grandfather got off the boat first. They went to talk to the villagers. Then everyone walked back to the *Avant*.

Kilian and Higgins helped Murgatroyd to get off the boat. As Murgatroyd walked away from the *Avant*, Monsieur Patient took off his straw hat and said, 'Salut, Mâitre.'

The villagers repeated his words. 'Salut, Mâitre, salut,' they said quietly.

'What are they saying?' asked Higgins.

'They're talking to Mr Murgatroyd,' said Kilian. 'They're calling him a master, a great fisherman.'

'Because I caught the Emperor?' asked Murgatroyd.

'No! Because you gave him his life,' said Kilian.

Kilian and Higgins took Murgatroyd to the small hospital in the village. A young Indian doctor put some bandages on Murgatroyd's hands.

At nine o'clock, Monsieur Patient came to the hospital. He and Murgatroyd talked for half an hour.

It was ten o'clock when Murgatroyd and Higgins walked

through the doors of the Hotel St Geran. Murgatroyd was very tired. His skin was burnt by the sun. Both his hands were covered with white bandages.

Harry Foster, the Australian, held up a glass of beer. 'Well done!' he said. He was drunk again.

Then Edna Murgatroyd came downstairs. She had curlers[49] in her hair. She was very angry.

'Murgatroyd!' Edna shouted. She always called her husband 'Murgatroyd' when she was angry. 'Where have you been? You look terrible!'

Murgatroyd looked at his wife. The curlers in her hair were like snakes. Suddenly, he shouted at her.

'And you look terrible too, Edna! Be quiet or go to bed!'

Edna Murgatroyd's mouth opened but she said nothing. She had been married to Roger Murgatroyd for twenty-five years and he had never shouted at her.

'Edna, for twenty-five years you have made me unhappy,' Murgatroyd said to his wife. 'You have often said that you wanted to go to live with your sister. Well, now you *can* go to live with her. You are free. I shall not return to England with you tomorrow.'

A crowd of people had come from the hotel bar. They stood with Harry Foster and they looked at Roger Murgatroyd.

'Have you forgotten your job at the bank?' asked Higgins. 'You can't leave the bank, Murgatroyd. How will you earn money? How will you live?'

'Edna can have our house and everything in it,' said Murgatroyd. 'I have a little money. I'm going to buy Monsieur Patient's boat and a small house on the beach here. I will learn about the sea and about fishing. Monsieur Patient will teach me. We will go game-fishing with the tourists who come here, to Mauritius. They will pay us well.'

'But – the bank!' said Higgins.

'And me. Have you forgotten about me?' Edna asked angrily.

Roger Murgatroyd thought for a moment, then he said, 'To hell with[50] the bank! And to hell with you, Edna!'

And Murgatroyd started to walk towards the hotel bar. The crowd of people with Harry Foster followed him. They laughed and shouted.

Harry Foster smiled and held up his glass of beer. 'Good on yer, Murgatroyd!' he said.

THERE ARE NO SNAKES IN IRELAND[51]

Mr McQueen sat in his small office in Bangor, in Northern Ireland. He looked at the young Indian man who was sitting on the other side of the desk. McQueen hired workmen to work on building sites. This young Indian wanted a job.

'Have you worked on a building site before?' McQueen asked the young man.

'No,' answered the young Indian. 'I am a medical student in Belfast. I am studying medicine at the university. I'm going to be a doctor. I must work during the summer vacation[52]. I must earn some money so that I can finish my studies. I need a job. Please, will you hire me?'

McQueen was a kind man. He wanted to help the young medical student. But he had never hired an Indian before. He usually hired men who had been born in Northern Ireland. Some of these Irishmen did not like foreigners.

'You know that the work is very hard, don't you?' McQueen said.

'Yes, sir,' answered the medical student.

'It's a cash-and-no-questions job,' said McQueen. 'Do you understand me?'

'No, not really, sir.'

'Cash-and-no-questions means that I will pay you every week. I will pay you cash. I won't pay any tax to the government. I won't pay any tax and *you* won't pay any tax. Don't tell anybody that you have a job. Don't ask any questions and everyone will be happy.'

McQueen was saying that the young man would be breaking the law[53], and McQueen would be breaking the law too.
The work would be dirty and dangerous. And it would have
to be done quickly. But the young man would earn a lot of
money.

The student nodded his head and said, 'Yes. I understand.'

McQueen picked up a pen. 'What's your name?' he asked.

'Harkishan Ram Lal,' replied the student.

'OK,' said McQueen, 'I'll call you Ram. Be outside the
railway station at six-thirty on Monday morning, Ram.'

Ram Lal left Mr McQueen's office and he went by train to
Belfast. He lived in Belfast, in a room near the university. He
had lived there for four years, while he was studying to be a
doctor. But now, during this summer vacation, he would
have to start working in Bangor at six-thirty every morning.
So he decided to move to Bangor for the summer.

The young man put some clothes in his suitcase and then
he took a train back to Bangor. He quickly found a cheap[54]
room near the railway station.

'One more year of studies,' he thought. 'In one year, I
will have finished my studies here. Then I will go back to
India. I will be a doctor.'

At six-thirty, the next morning, Ram Lal waited outside the
railway station.

A dozen other men were standing outside the station.
Most of them were carrying plastic lunch-boxes[55]. Ram Lal
went to stand with the other men. They were all waiting for
the foreman – Billie Cameron.

Billie Cameron arrived in an old truck. He was a huge
man. He was two metres tall and he weighed one hundred

and twenty kilos. So everyone called him 'Big Billie'.

'Get into the back of the truck!' Big Billie shouted at the men. Then he looked at Ram Lal. 'Get in the truck with the others,' he said.

The men sat on wooden seats in the back of the truck. The engine made a loud noise and the old truck moved off down the street.

The man who sat opposite Ram Lal had bright blue eyes and a friendly face. He said that his name was Tommy Burns.

'Where are you from?' he asked the student.

'India,' replied Ram Lal. 'The Punjab.'

'Well, which place?' asked Tommy Burns. 'India or the Punjab?'

Ram Lal smiled. 'The Punjab is part of India, Tommy,' he explained.

Tommy Burns had never left Northern Ireland. And he had never met anyone from India.

'Our new man is a long way from home,' he said to the other workmen.

'Aye. But why is he here?' Big Billie called out. 'Why isn't he working in India?'

'Why *are* you in Northern Ireland?' asked Tommy Burns.

'I'm a medical student at Belfast University,' Ram Lal replied. 'I came to Northern Ireland in 1971. Next year, I will qualify as[56] a doctor.'

'So, you're a doctor.' Tommy Burns was pleased. 'If anyone is hurt on the building site, you will help them, Ram.'

'I won't let him touch me!' Big Billie said loudly.

After that, all the men were silent. They were afraid of Big Billie.

Soon, the truck arrived at the building site and the men

got out. They were near a river. Ram Lal saw an old factory. There were trees around it. There were no houses or shops. There was nowhere to buy food.

Ram Lal understood that they had not come to build anything. They were going to knock down this old factory.

The owner of the factory wanted the job to be done quickly and cheaply. He did not want to pay for bulldozers or any other machines. The workmen were going to knock down the factory with big hammers and iron bars.

The men took the hammers and bars from the truck and they started to work.

The work was very hard. The sun was hot and the air was dusty. Before the end of the morning, Ram Lal was tired. He was also hungry.

At midday, everyone stopped working. The other men opened their plastic lunch-boxes and took out their food.

'Didn't you bring any sandwiches?' Tommy Burns asked Ram Lal.

'No,' said the young medical student. 'I'll bring a lunch-box tomorrow.'

Ram Lal had nothing to eat but there was plenty of tea to drink. The men made a fire and they boiled water in a kettle. They made tea and drank it out of metal mugs. Tommy had two mugs and he gave one to Ram Lal. But the tea was sweet and it had milk in it. Ram Lal did not like it.

Tommy held out his lunch-box towards the young Indian. 'Here, take a sandwich,' he said.

'The foreigner should bring his own sandwiches!' shouted Big Billie Cameron.

Tommy Burns looked down at the ground. Everyone was afraid of Big Billie.

'Thank you, but I'm not hungry,' Ram Lal said to Tommy.

The next day, he brought his own lunch in a red metal lunch-box.

But Ram Lal did not like his job. By the end of every day, his arms and legs were aching and he was very, very tired. And the student did not like Big Billie Cameron. But he needed the money.

That week, the foreman made Ram Lal do the difficult and dangerous work. Ram Lal did not like high places, but Big Billie told him to climb onto the factory roof.

Soon, the roof was knocked down. Next, the workmen started to knock down the walls. Ram Lal had to climb to the top of the walls.

On Saturday morning, the men were sitting down and drinking their tea.

'This is what we'll do next,' Big Billie said. 'We'll knock down that big wall over there. We must start at the top.'

He pointed to the top of the wall and he spoke to Ram Lal. 'I want you to go up there,' he said.

Ram Lal looked at the wall which Big Billie was pointing to. The wall was cracked[57] near the bottom. The wall was very weak.

'That wall is going to fall down,' Ram Lal said. 'If it falls, then I will fall too.'

'Don't tell me how to do this job, you stupid foreigner!' Big Billie shouted. He started to walk away.

Ram Lal stood up. He was very angry.

'Mr Cameron,' Ram Lal shouted. 'I am a stranger in your country but I am not stupid. Please do not insult[58] me!'

Big Billie turned round. He was surprised. All the men were surprised. No one spoke to Big Billie like that.

Big Billie walked up to Ram Lal and hit him hard on the side of his head. Ram Lal fell to the ground. Tommy Burns spoke quietly to him.

'Stay there,' said Tommy. 'He'll kill you if you get up.'

Ram Lal could not get up. When he tried to stand, he felt weak and dizzy. Finally, he did get up and he went back to his work. He said nothing and no one else spoke to him for the rest of the day.

———

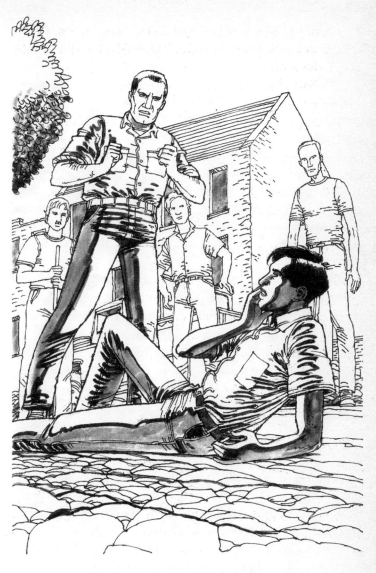

Big Billie hit him hard on the side of the head.
Ram Lal fell to the ground.

That night, Ram Lal sat in his room near the station. He was very angry. He wanted to leave his job on the building site. But he needed the money – he could not leave.

What could he do? He had been insulted. And Big Billie had hit him very hard. The foreman might have killed him. Now, the young Indian wanted to kill Big Billie Cameron.

Suddenly, Ram Lal heard thunder. A storm was beginning. Loud thunder made the house shake and lightning lit up the student's small room.

The young man's dressing-gown[59] was hanging on the back of the door. It had a belt made of thick cord. When the lightning flashed, it lit up the back of the door. The dressing-gown cord looked like a snake. Suddenly, Ram Lal had an idea.

The next day was Sunday. Ram Lal did not have to go to work. He went to Belfast to visit a friend. His friend was another Indian medical student. He came from a rich family.

'My father is ill,' Ram Lal said to his friend. 'I must go to India to see him. Will you lend me some money? I need to buy a ticket for the plane.'

The rich student liked Ram Lal very much. He knew that Ram Lal would repay the money.

'I will go to the bank tomorrow morning,' he said. 'Meet me at the bank at nine forty-five. I will give you the money then.'

Ram Lal thanked his friend and he took the train back to Bangor.

The next morning, the young man went to Mr McQueen's office. Ram Lal was carrying a suitcase.

'Mr McQueen,' said Ram Lal, 'I cannot go to the building site today. My father is ill. I must go to India for a few days.

But I want to work for you again when I return. I will go to India this afternoon and I will come back before the end of the week. Please, will you give me a job again next week?'

'OK, Ram,' said Mr McQueen. 'You can have your job again when you come back. I won't pay you for the days when you are away. And there are some things that you must do – some conditions. You must come back to Ireland on Friday. And you must start work again on Saturday.'

'Thank you very much, Mr McQueen,' said Ram Lal.

Ram Lal left Mr McQueen's office and went quickly to the station. He took a train to Belfast. He was going to meet his friend near the bank. By ten o'clock, Ram Lal had the money for his journey and he was travelling to the airport.

At the airport, Ram Lal bought a return ticket to Bombay, then he took a plane to London. At London airport, he took the flight to Bombay. It was Tuesday morning when he arrived in the city of Bombay. But he did not travel on to the Punjab.

———

Ram Lal knew a man in Bombay whose name was Mr Chatterjee. Mr Chatterjee had a shop. He sold animals. Some of the animals were bought by scientists and medical students. Mr Chatterjee had many snakes in his shop.

On Wednesday morning, Ram Lal went to visit him. He asked Mr Chatterjee a question.

'Ah, yes,' said Mr Chatterjee, 'the Indian Viper. Yes, I have one. It is a small and dangerous snake. It is poisonous. Indian Vipers often bite men and can kill a man quickly. Sometimes, people do not know that a snake has bitten them. There is no pain, but a person who is bitten dies in four hours. I will sell you the viper for 350 rupees[60].'

Mr Chatterjee put the small snake into a small wooden box. The box had a few small holes in it. The snake could live in the box for many days, without food and water. Ram Lal gave Mr Chatterjee 350 rupees and he left the shop.

The next day, Ram Lal put the wooden box into his suit-case. He put some clothes on top of the box and he closed the case. He remembered Mr McQueen's conditions. He went to the airport and he took a plane to London. On Friday afternoon, the young Indian was back in Bangor.

————

On Saturday morning, Ram Lal went to work on the building site. Inside his red metal lunch-box was the small snake.

Big Billie Cameron always came to the building site in a thick black jacket. This Saturday morning, the weather was very hot. Big Billie took off his jacket when he started work-ing and he hung it on a tree.

All morning, the men worked hard. They moved the bricks from the broken walls to some trucks. The trucks took the bricks away.

When no one was watching him, Ram Lal put the snake into a pocket of Big Billie's jacket. It was the pocket where the foreman kept his cigarettes.

The men stopped working at midday. They sat down and they ate their sandwiches and drank their tea. Then Big Billie stood up and put his hand into his jacket pocket. He took out a packet of cigarettes. Suddenly, he saw that Ram Lal was looking at him.

'Why are you staring at me?' Big Billie shouted.

Ram Lal said nothing. He looked at the foreman's jacket.

Ram Lal had thought that the snake would bite Big Billie. He had thought that the foreman would shout. He had thought that Big Billie would throw the little snake onto the ground. Ram Lal was going to stamp his foot on the viper and kill it. He was going to throw the snake's body into the river.

51

But nothing happened. Where *was* the viper? Why had it not bitten Big Billie? Ram Lal worried about the snake for the rest of the day.

———

In the evening, Big Billie went home and hung his jacket on the back of his kitchen door. He did not wear the jacket on Sunday.

On Monday morning, he saw that the jacket had fallen onto the kitchen floor. The cloth of the jacket was moving! Then he saw a small creature coming out of a pocket. The creature looked like a snake.

'But there are no snakes in Ireland,' Big Billie thought. 'This little creature must be a lizard[61]. It can't be a snake!'

Big Billie was going to stamp his foot on the lizard and kill it. But then he had an idea. He got an empty box. Very carefully, he picked up the creature and he put it into the box.

That morning, at the building site, the workmen were burning the wood from the factory's roof. Big Billie was happy. The big foreman laughed with all the workmen and he told them jokes.

But Ram Lal was *not* happy. He was afraid.

Ram Lal's idea had not been a good one. For two days, he had worried about the snake. It was a poisonous viper. Every year, many people in India were bitten by vipers and they died. *This* snake might kill somebody in Northern Ireland. It *might* kill Big Billie, but it *might* kill somebody else!

The student did not see Big Billie put something in his red metal lunch-box. The other men saw what Big Billie did. They knew that the foreman was going to trick Ram Lal. They smiled at each other.

At midday, everyone sat on the ground to eat their lunch.

Big Billy put something in Ram Lal's lunch-box.

The Irishmen looked at Ram Lal. They were waiting for something to happen but Ram Lal did not know this. He took the lid off his red lunch-box. Inside the box, he saw the Indian viper. It was going to bite him!

The student threw the box into the air and jumped up. He shouted, 'Snake! A poisonous snake! Kill it quickly!'

The other men laughed and laughed. Big Billie laughed more than all the others. Ram Lal's food had fallen onto the dusty ground beside the foreman. Big Billie spoke to Ram Lal.

'You stupid foreigner,' he said, 'don't you know that there are no snakes in Ireland? Now you can't eat your lunch!'

Big Billie did not feel the small snake on his right hand. He did not feel it bite him. And a few minutes later, the foreman stood up and said, 'Let's start working again.'

Soon all the men were working. Ram Lal worked silently. He was angry and he was worried. His plan had gone wrong.

After three hours, the foreman stopped working. 'I feel ill,' he said. He put his hands over his face. 'I must sit down.'

Soon, Big Billie fell asleep. The other men went on working for an hour.

At half-past four, everybody stopped working. Suddenly, one of the men shouted, 'Big Billie is ill! He won't wake up. We must take him to the hospital. We need an ambulance.'

The man got into the truck and drove away. He was going to find a telephone. He was going to call an ambulance.

'You're a doctor, Ram,' Tommy Burns said to Ram Lal. 'What's wrong with Big Billie?'

Ram Lal knew what was wrong with the foreman. He knew that Big Billie was dead.

———

Big Billie was dead when the ambulance got to the hospital.

54

The doctors at the hospital said that he had died from a stroke[62].

'He worked too long in the hot sun,' one of the doctors said. 'That's why he died.'

A few days later, the job on the building site was finished. But the next Sunday, Ram Lal went to the building site again. He went alone. He stood in the place where Big Billie Cameron had died.

Ram Lal had killed the big foreman. But soon, he would qualify as a doctor. Then he would help to *save* lives.

But where was the snake? Where had the viper gone? It could not live long in this cold land. It would die in the winter.

'Are you listening, snake?' Ram Lal said loudly. 'You have killed here, and you will die here. You will die alone, because there are no snakes in Ireland.'

But the snake was not listening. She was busy. She was taking care of her babies.

Points for Understanding

USED IN EVIDENCE

1 Dublin City Council was going to build a new shopping centre in Mayo Road. Why did the council ask the police for help?

2 When Bill Hanley arrived in Mayo Road, he saw two newspaper reporters. Was he happy to see them? Why/why not?

3 A man in the crowd, in Mayo Road, called out, 'Is there some treasure in there?' Why did he ask this question?

4 How was the pathologist going to help Hanley's investigation?

5 The pathologist phoned Hanley. He said that the body was a mummy.
   (a) What did he mean?
   (b) What had happened to the body?

6 What did Hanley learn from the British Army pay book which was found in Mr Larkin's house?

7 Who was Major Dawkins? How did he help Hanley?

8 Why was Mrs Moran certain about the date when Mrs Larkin disappeared?

9 Why did Hanley decide to charge Mr Larkin with the murder of his wife?

10 The day after the body was found, the pathologist gave Hanley some information. And the deeds of the house had given Hanley some information. What did all this information tell Hanley about the body and about Herbert Larkin?

11 Hanley asked the sergeant, 'Who was the man who lived at 38 Mayo Road before the Larkins?'
   What did Hanley think about the body when he had heard the sergeant's reply?

12 Mr Larkin watched the bulldozer at the building site. Then he smiled and he walked back to his new home.
   Why do you think that Mr Larkin smiled?

THE EMPEROR

1 Mrs Murgatroyd was always complaining.
What is the meaning of 'complain'?

2 What did Mrs Murgatroyd complain about
(a) in the taxi?
(b) when she arrived at the hotel?

3 'So – Murgatroyd of the Midland and Higgins from Head
Office,' said Harry Foster.
(a) What was he talking about?
(b) Why did he think that these words were funny?

4 Roger looked out of the window of the hotel room and he felt
happy. What did he like about Mauritius?

5 Every day, the Murgatroyds did the same things. Did Edna stop
complaining?

6 Roger Murgatroyd and John Higgins went fishing in the *Avant*.
There was a special seat at the back of the boat. What was the
seat for?

7 There was a bucket of squid in the *Avant*. What were the squid
for?

8 There was a harness fixed to the fishing-seat. What was this
harness for?

9 How long did Roger Murgatroyd fight the Emperor?

10 At last, Roger reeled in the huge Marlin. But he did not let
Jean-Paul kill it. Why do you think that he did not want the
fish to be killed?

11 Roger told Edna that he had talked with Monsieur Patient.
What had they talked about?

12 What are Roger's plans for the future now?

13 When she heard Roger's plans, Edna was not happy. She wanted to complain but she could not. Why not?

14 The other hotel guests laughed and shouted. Why do you think
that they did this?

THERE ARE NO SNAKES IN IRELAND

1 What is a 'cash-and-no-questions' job?
2 Ram Lal was going to break the law. How and why?
3 In which year was Ram Lal going to qualify as a doctor?
4 The men were going to a 'building site'.
    (a) Were they going to build anything?
    (b) What job were they going to do?
5 'Thank you, but I am not hungry,' Ram Lal said to Tommy
    Burns. Do you think that this was true?
6 The foreman told Ram Lal to climb up onto the wall. Ram Lal
    did not want to do this. Why not?
7 In the evening there was a storm. Suddenly, Ram Lal had an
    idea.
    (a) What gave him the idea?
    (b) What do you think the idea was?
8 'My father is ill,' Ram Lal said to his friend. Was he telling the
    truth?
9 Ram Lal told Mr McQueen that he had to go to India. Mr
    McQueen told the student that he could come back to his job.
    But there were some conditions. What were these conditions?
10 Mr Chatterjee gave Ram Lal some information about the snake.
    What did he say about it?
11 On Saturday, Ram Lal went to the building site with the other
    men. He took the snake with him. Why?
12 Ram Lal's plan did not succeed on Saturday. Why not?
13 On Monday morning, Big Billie had a surprise. What was it?
14 The surprise gave Billie an idea. What was his idea?
15 On Monday morning, Ram Lal was not happy. Why not?
16 The doctors said that Big Billie had worked too long in the hot
    sun and that he had had a stroke. What had really happened?
17 The next Sunday, Ram Lal returned to the building site alone.
    He spoke to the snake. Were his words true?

Glossary

1 **Used in Evidence** (page 7)
   when a policeman arrests someone, he uses these words. He says,
   'Anything that you say will be used in evidence in a court of law.'
   This means that the court will be told what the person said when
   they were arrested.
2 **Dublin City Council** (page 7)
   the people who take care of a city or a town are the members of
   its council. A city council has many departments. Each department has a special job. For example, there are departments which
   take care of old people, children and hospitals.
3 **knocked down** (page 7)
   houses are knocked down to destroy them. Workers hit the walls
   with hammers or push them over with machines.
4 **building site** (page 7)
   a place where workmen are building or knocking down houses,
   shops, factories or building roads. (see No.3)
5 **tarmac** (page 7)
   when tar is hot, it is a thick black liquid. Small pieces of stone
   are added to hot tar to make tarmac. Flat ground is covered with
   hot tarmac to make roads and car parks. When it is cold, tarmac
   becomes hard and strong.
6 **in charge of** (page 8)
   when someone is in charge of other people, they tell the other
   people what things they must do or how to do things.
7 **muddy** (page 8)
   when the ground becomes very soft and wet, it is *muddy*.
8 **social workers** (page 8)
   officials who take care of people who are old, ill or in trouble.
9 **Housing Department** (page 8)
   the department of a council which builds houses for people and
   decides who can live in them. (see No.2)
10 **order from the court** (page 9)
   the council asked a judge in a court of law about Mr Larkin. The
   judge has said that Mr Larkin must leave his house. The judge
   has given the council a document – an order – which says this.

11 *fireplace and chimney* (page 12)
a *chimney* is a tall tube, made of bricks, which is built against the wall of a room. A fire burns in a hole at the bottom of this chimney – this is the *fireplace*. Smoke from the fire goes up the chimney and not into the room.

12 *mortuary* (page 12)
a place where the bodies of dead people are kept before they are buried.

13 *investigation* (page 12)
when somebody does something which is against the law, they commit a crime. The police try to find out who has committed a crime. This police work is called an *investigation*.

14 *suspect* (page 12)
if the police think that a person has done something wrong, that person is a *suspect*.

15 *interview room* (page 14)
a room in a police station where policemen talk to people about crimes.

16 *police pathologist* (page 14)
a scientist who works for the police. A pathologist looks carefully at the bodies of dead people and the places where the bodies are found. The pathologist then reports to the police.

17 *post-mortem examination* (page 14)
post-mortem = after death (Latin). The pathologist does many tests on a dead body and looks carefully at the inside and the outside of the body. This examination tells the pathologist how the person died.

18 *mummy* (page 15)
a body which has been dead for a long time and is completely dried. In Egypt, thousands of years ago, the bodies of important people were made into mummies.

19 *British Embassy* (page 17)
a building in a foreign country where officials of the British government work.

20 *military attaché* (page 17)
a soldier who works as an official in an embassy.

21 *deeds* (page 17)
papers which give the names of all the people who buy and sell that house.

22 **security guard** (page 17)
someone who is paid to guard a building or a piece of land.
23 **retire** (page 17)
when people are old, they leave their jobs and stop working.
They *retire* from work.
24 **President John F. Kennedy** (page 18)
President of the USA, 1961–1963. He was shot dead in Dallas,
Texas, on 22 November 1963.
25 **I charge you with...** (page 20)
when a policeman believes that someone has committed a crime,
he uses these words. Then that person will have a trial in a court
of law.
26 **concrete** (page 20)
a mixture of sand, small stones, cement and water. When it dries,
concrete becomes very hard and strong. It is used to make roads
and the walls of buildings.
27 **Second World War** (page 21)
the war of 1939–1945. Germany, Italy and Japan fought several
other European countries, the USA and the USSR. The British
and German armies fought many battles in Egypt.
28 **prison camp** (page 21)
if soldiers were prisoners after a battle, they were kept in a prison
camp.
29 **foreman** (page 22)
the person in charge of the workers on a building site. (see Nos. 4
and 6)
30 **bulldozer** (page 23)
a large machine which is used on building sites. It is used to
move earth, to spread tarmac and to knock down low walls.
31 **employee** (page 24)
someone who works for a person or for a company.
32 **shorts** (page 25)
trousers with short legs which are worn in hot weather.
33 **accent** (page 25)
people from different countries speak the same language but with
different sounds. These sounds are called an *accent*. People from
Australia speak English with an Australian accent.
34 **colleague** (page 25)
when somebody works with another person, that person is his
colleague.

35 **branch** (page 27)
a bank is a large company which takes care of people's money. It
has a head office, where the most important people work. And it
has smaller offices – or branches – in many towns.

36 **Good on yer!** (page 27)
= Good on you! When an Australian says this, he means, 'You
are a clever person!' or 'You have done that well!'

37 **sun-tan oil** (page 28)
oil which you put on your body to stop the heat of the sun burning your skin.

38 **romantic novels** (page 28)
stories which are about people falling in love and getting married.

39 **hire** (page 28)
to *hire* someone is to pay someone to do a job. To hire something,
is to pay someone to use something they own – for example, a
car, a boat or a machine.

40 **I don't care** (page 29)
Roger has decided that he will do what he wants to do. He will
not worry about what his wife wants to do.

41 **guide** (page 29)
someone whose job is to take people to places where they have
never been and to show them how to do things.

42 **seventies** (page 29)
someone in his seventies is between 70 and 79 years old.

43 **tool-box** (page 30)
a metal or wooden box which contains equipment needed for a
machine or for a sport.

44 **squid** (page 30)
creatures which live in the sea. They have soft bodies and eight
legs. 'Squid' is both a singular word and a plural word.

45 **reel** (page 30)
a metal wheel which is fixed to a fishing rod. It holds the fishing
line. The fisherman turns a handle on the reel in one direction
to let out some line. He turns it in the other direction to bring
the line back – to *reel* in.

46 **wire-cutters** (page 32)
a sharp tool – like scissors – used for cutting metal wire.

47 **bleed** (page 36)
blood was coming from Roger's hands.

48 **dizzy** (page 38)
    when you are *dizzy* you cannot stand up or see easily.
49 **curlers** (page 39)
    plastic or metal tubes which women sometimes put in their hair
    when it is wet. When the hair dries, it *curls*.
50 **To hell with...** (page 40)
    a very strong way of saying that you do not care about someone
    or something.
51 **There Are No Snakes in Ireland** (page 41)
    See the *Note About These Stories* on page 4.
52 **summer vacation** (page 41)
    in the UK, students do not study during the months of July, August
    and September. They have a holiday or vacation, at this time.
53 **break the law** (page 42)
    do something which is against the law – something which the
    law says you must not do.
54 **cheap** (page 42)
    not expensive. Ram does not pay much money to live in this room.
55 **lunch-box** (page 42)
    a box with a lid, which holds food.
56 **qualify as** (page 43)
    when medical students have finished their studies and they have
    passed all their exams, they *qualify as* doctors. Then they can
    take care of sick people.
57 **cracked** (page 46)
    a crack in a wall is a place where the bricks are no longer fixed to
    each other. Something with a crack in it is *cracked*.
58 **insult** (page 46)
    to say something to someone which is rude and untrue.
59 **dressing-gown** (page 48)
    a long, loose coat with a belt. Dressing-gowns are worn over
    nightclothes.
60 **rupee** (page 49)
    the money which is used in India.
61 **lizard** (page 52)
    lizards are animals like snakes. But they have four legs and a long
    tail. They usually live in warm, dry grass.
62 **stroke** (page 55)
    a sudden illness in the brain. Sometimes, people who have
    strokes cannot see or hear or move. Sometimes, they die.

Macmillan Heinemann English Language Teaching, Oxford

A division of Macmillan Publishers Limited

Companies and representatives throughout the world

ISBN 0 435 27255 1

Heinemann is a registered trademark of Reed Educational and Professional Publishing Limited

The stories 'Used In Evidence', 'There Are No Snakes In Ireland' and 'The Emperor' were first published in Great Britain in the collection of short stories entitled *No Comebacks* by Frederick Forsyth (Century Hutchinson Ltd 1982)

© Frederick Forsyth 1972, 1973, 1979, 1982
The right of Frederick Forsyth to be identified as author of this work has been asserted by him in accordance with Copyright, Designs and Patents Act, 1988

These retold versions by Stephen Colbourn of 'Used in Evidence', 'There Are No Snakes in Ireland' and 'The Emperor' for Heinemann Guided Readers
Text © Macmillan Publishers Limited 1998
Design and illustration © Macmillan Publishers Limited 1998

This edition first published 1998

Illustrated by David Cuzik
Typography by Adrian Hodgkins
Designed by Sue Vaudin
Cover by Tim Jonke and Marketplace Design
Typeset in 11/13.5pt Goudy

Printed and bound in Spain by Mateu Cromo

99 00 01 02 10 9 8 7 6 5 4 3 2